THE UNIVERSITY OF
WINCHESTER

THE PIG

BY

PETER LEWIN

*"The poems in 'The Pig' represent a sort of
Peter Lewin Top Fifty, many years in the making and a
pleasure to read. Lewin uses words sparingly but to
great effect. He can convey a whole set of beliefs in one
or two lines of dialogue. Poems such as
'Knightwood' and 'Dis Morning Dis Voice Sez'
sound like the rare kind, those that were crying out for
the right person to come along and write them.
Lewin can also be very funny when he chooses, using
great comic timing and a perfect deadpan delivery in
pieces such as 'Spud Taylor' and 'The Toilet Seat.'
When I read the last poem in this book I wished there
were more and I had to re-read them all instead.
Here's one book of poems that won't make you feel like
smacking the poet."*

GEOFF HATTERSLEY

THE PIG
BY
PETER LEWIN

-FLUX GALLERY PRESS-

Copyright © 2006 Peter Lewin

✫

Poem titles set in 12pt / 10pt caps Palatino Linotype Bold
The poems are set in 10pt Palatino Linotype Bold / Bold Italic

✫

Cover Photography by Daniel Lyons
"A Pig Hello" to Marylin & Denise at Home Farm,
Temple Newsam.
Cover Layout / Typography by John Brownlee

Published by
Flux Gallery Press
16a Midland Road
LEEDS LS6 1BQ

☎ 0113 2304397
www.fluxgallerypress.co.uk

First published 2006

ISBN 0-9550158-6-3

Printed & bound by
BEACON DM, Valley Road Business Park,
Keighley. BD21 4LY

- A C K N O W L E D G E M E N T S -

Several of these poems appeared in the previous Peter Lewin publications :

Knightwood	*(Dog Press, 1997)*
Temperature of Stars	*(Glass Head Press, 2002)*
Silverdale	*(Kendall Press, 2003)*
Lost Passports	*(Troubador, 2005)*

Other poems have appeared in the following magazines :

Albert Poets Anthologies, Brando's Hat, Dog, Dreamcatcher, Headlock, Inago (USA), Iota, Obsessed by Pipework, Pearl (USA), Pennine Platform, Poetry and Audience (Leeds University), Poetry Monthly, Poetry Nottingham, Purple Patch, Reater, Rialto, Scratch, Smith's Knoll, The Echo Room, The Journal, The New Writer, The Penniless Press, The Slab, The Wide Skirt, T.O.P.S., Yellow Crane.

- D E D I C A T I O N S -

"Bird" *dedicated to* William Park
"The Pig" *dedicated to* Dan Lyons
"Eine Kleine Nachtmusik *dedicated to* Mary T. Parry
"Saxophone" *dedicated to* Andrew Oldham
"Hyacinths" *dedicated to* Kevin Draper
"Goldwing And Swallow" *dedicated to* Milner Place
"Night Coach" *dedicated to* Ian Parks
"The Toilet Seat" *dedicated to* Shane Rhodes
"The Chippy" *dedicated to* Moniza Alvi
"Strawberries" *dedicated to* David Crystal

For
Carolyn Ann Lewin : (Titch).
My family and friends.

-CONTENTS-

BIRD

Wore a woolly hat in summer.
Slow, odd, old she was,
Feeding the body of Christ.

Like food to bird tables,
Flowering like mad
inventions....snowing from elms.

Strange....it was strange
Summer didn't seem to mind.
Feathered bouquets....her white hands.

ON A SLEEPING MAN'S FACE

On a sleeping man's face,
mottled moonlight played
like an old projector.
A shotgun rang-out shooting a pheasant
that was beautiful.

Film ran on, on windy cloud-shadows,
a father-figure walked on: Clark Gable,
but in cool dead-certainty.
A golden-curled child ran by his side
looking like a dog looking at a god,
coming to heel, to fetch, sit and drop....

A caption read; *A Gun's Face Can Never Be Holy.*

A few fields and hedges later, a close-up
caught, captured the child's confusion, the downwards
focus on some drowned kittens, outside a back door,
in a tin bucket, in clear water, in a tied stocking,
like a lumpy bumpy black Christmas,
covered with stone.

The film putters on into hushed dark confidences
showing the father, showing the son, how to strangle
a rabbit, in a net, in the wood,
making it pee yellow and strong.

THE PIG

Uncles and Aunts in the front room,
a 1950's Christmas time,
lots of balloon-backed chairs
with gothic carved demon faces,
lots of seats, lots of family.

My out-of-sight father
cutting up the huge white stone
of pig: its eyes closed down.
I casually wander in
attracted to this magnet man,

his deftness with the bone-
handled kitchen knife....
See him gouge out the pig's
eye like a miniature jellyfish.
He plops it neatly in my palm.

1953

Mum and Dad took me to the small town pictures
On a dark rainy night. I'd be seven - can't remember the film

But I remembered the newsreel - the cock a doodle doo
(Didn't know why) : the bleary boulibasse-eyed man
    who died -

Swarthy in the mackintosh, storming wildly out from the
    silver screen,
Over the short back and sides....the stalls. My school kid
    basin cut,

My bruised nettled knees....over the Park Drive and
    Woodbine haze.
Over the smeared lipsticks and theatre smells....

Over the drying overcoats and tweed postwar....over
    the rustle
Of my Smith's crisps - the blue twist bag on the floor -
    a Nuttall's Mintoe

Mum saying he was a bad lot, a womaniser, a man not to be
    trusted.
But the man's eyes were saying something I couldn't quite
    grasp then,

Or read their situations....I focussed on the moon face,
    the stub nose.
The glaring lights, a wet New York - the black and white of
    it....

The neon signs his twilight. Cold figures running like
    baddies -
Collars to the wind....flash bulbs snuffing out.

The ambulance quivers to a halt -
Darkness clutching the coldness of its inner wheels.

Faces gawp at the prince of the apple towns
Who sang like the sea in his chains.

BEFORE THE YO-YO

1950 something, and all the kids
were doing it: floating tea spoons
on the tops of their cups of tea

watching it fill and swirl
then plunge fast to the bottom
like the ship on The Pathe News.

You'll find that front page
lining old chests or old cupboards:
The Captain with death in his eyes

going down, not knowing he was
starting a schoolboy craze.

SAY CHEESE 1957

The dog lead catches her face,
her pigtails whip the walls
as she slumps against plaster.
Dad smiles, adjusts his trilby
at a slight angle in the mirror;
brushes his moustache with forefinger.

He pushes me out of the way.
The door slams:
Dickie Valentine brylcreem boy
sings a love song on the television
in the back room over coconut-matting.
A goldfish blinks in a weedless bowl.

My sister sits in a chair head slumped
her pigtails dangle down, ribbons loose.
I make her cheese on toast
with Kraft Cheese slices;
I'm an expert at it.
Watching it bubble like blisters.

EINE KLEINE NACHTMUSIK

201's ajar, a slant of light;
the eye of a nightmare.
Giant sunflower broken
on the landing;
petals on the stairs.
Children traumatised:
7 year old Mary
corkscrew golden hair
torn dress; yellow
petal in hand -
leaning by the door:
Washed out, blood drained.

Jane 6, ripped skirt;
hair rippling upwards:
No apples in the cheek -
just a face of grief.
The sunflower a crucified
Christ cut down from Heaven.

Someone's dying out
of frame in room 209.
In 207 a raven's pecked
out teddy's brown eyes.
Outside a snowstorm;
and the virgins are the
bone-chimes of tomorrow.

No Message

He always had this thing
about locking doors.
It used to wind me up
when I couldn't get in
or out without my keys.

Once he found out
I'd left the front door
open all night,
didn't speak to me for a week.

Not long after,
I came home one teatime -
chips frying, bread buttered,
table set, eggs cracked
in the bowl, ready for the pan.

His pint of tea steaming
on the sink, no sign of him
then or ever.

MISTRESS

So....you think he was a really nice bloke.
A bit of a character, eh ! That was how
you put it. I must admit he was a
good talker and listener, most good con-men
are. Now, I am not disputing he wasn't
clever, he was a cracker with words:
A wonderful flatterer. You're not the first
woman to fall for the silver-tongued man.
Yes....I can see you look at me with
disbelief - you think I am talking through
my arse.
Yes....I can see he has done a good job
on you.
Now, listen to me, listen to me ! ! !
Not that you'll take any notice.
Yes, I know you were his mistress -
look, you've wasted your life,
been the painted woman.
He's kissed your lips black,
left you with nothing.
I overheard him once, blackmailing
his own mother, told her she
wouldn't see her grandchildren again
if she didn't go through with the
deal of selling her house - so he
could pay off his debts, secure
a new business - with the granny flat
at the bottom of the garden.
Look at me, you're dreaming again.
Listen, you still can't love the bastard
can you - can you ?

WALKING STICK

Up ahead people stream into church.
She smiles, tells me she can make it.
Gravel crunches beneath our feet;
light shines like the reflection
from a burnished cross.

Blue sky, snow clouds.
Daffodils move their heads
over gravestones.
Well-kept lawns incinerate my eyes.
Bells peal like they do at weddings.

She's using her walking stick,
the one I use now. I hold her.
She slumps to the ground.
We've nearly reached the church.
Everyone else is inside.

Try to open her eyes with thumb,
forefinger; only the whites show.
She's shrinking as I lift her,
place her in a cardboard box
to stop the cold biting into her.

The size of a doll now,
cover her with some red flannel,
just her pasty face showing;
slide her under the wooden seat
inside the church porch.

SAXOPHONE

I will be as loose as a rubber band
I will never be breathless, my heels will be wings
I will be running through the lily-of-the -valley

Along the pathways of Woodwell

I will see my parents' deaths, my relatives' deaths
I will see my old dog's death, my young cat's death
I will hold my breath and turn quite blue

I will feel Holy and without fear

I will be running towards my Mother's smile
I will be streaming tears behind a blue dream-saxophone
I will be thanking you all for inspiring me -

To sing some blues -

The mourning blues and daylight blues and evening blues
and midnight blues and twilight blues and colour blues
and everyone's there ripping up the floor.

HYACINTHS

Every year he would buy Hyacinth bulbs.
Occasionally I'd go with him
in his Austin Cambridge.
Being near him was good,
scent of Old Spice, St. Bruno.

Spent my childhood
looking out of front room windows,
always forgotten promises.
A day's fishing, the seaside,
a walk to Woodwell, the pictures.

Slender fingers pick out bulbs
from slanted trays, in the market.
At home lovingly plant them,
press soil with fingertips.

He re-lived lost days through grandchildren.
I used to wish on stars I could be one of them:
Casting their lines into rivers,
near meadows full of wildflowers.

GOLD-WING AND SWALLOW

He has been a wolf in a former life.
He waits outside your home.

He waits for the latch.
He likes to lick clean the bones.

He is the sliver of glass in your eye.
He loves the moth and the butterfly.

He will fry them bacon crisp then flambé,
he will serve them with Gold-Wing and Swallow.

He will shrivel the rose and dandelion.
He will bring the rain and the thunder.

He is the chill down your neck.
He is the spider on the virgin's flat belly.

He will have her with peaches and cream.
He is the blade of each flick knife.

He is the sperm at the crime scene,
the stare of the murdered girl.

The Flashbacks

Something about dancing zig-zags.
Something about flying through forests.

Something about being not one thing but two.
Something about having no charm.

Something about being half sting.
I pop toast in the toaster, light my first cigarette.

Something about honeysuckle, sweet lilac.
Something about disinfectant, silence.

SPUD TAYLOR

Are you Spud Taylor ?
No, I'm his younger brother.
God, you look just like him,
    we used to go to the same school.
Christ, that must be forty years ago.
He was always fighting.
Yeah, he was.
He gave me this bent nose.
Did he really ? he says laughing.

Yes, your brother knocked out my two front teeth.
Did he really ? he says laughing even louder.
Yes, your brother and I used to fight all the time.

I didn't tell him he was the school Psycho,
    that he picked fights for fun.
Most of our class had missing front teeth, bent noses,
    in fact,
I bet they're all out there now, doing the shopping,
following their girlfriends and wives around,
picking numbers for the lottery.
I remember that last fight, giving Spud a good few in the
    face,
next thing, though, he had his arm round my neck, landing
    uppercut after uppercut.

BARNEY ! BARNEY ! BARNEY ! the kids shouted.
Then we were getting six of the best, Spud loved all that
    lovely pain.

I remember walking home, my arse stinging, nose swelling,
   teeth missing, shirt covered in blood.
Now, here I am in Tesco's, having a conversation with his
   brother,
like we were long lost friends, well, I guess we are in a
   strange sort of way.

I went to the same school as his brother, lived in the same
town, used the same tuck shop, cinema, maybe warmed up
   on the same girls.
"Hell !" I say, really putting some feeling into it, "I'd really
   love to see Spud again, it'll be like a re-union....Good
old Spud and me !"

His brother is smiling, he's got Spud's face.
"He's got a fruit and veg on Headroomgate at Sweetsea," he
   replies.
He jots down the address and off he goes.

I look at his scrawled writing, and find myself thinking
about those cold school mornings, short trousers at thirteen,
school milk, banging my shins on iron desks, teachers
barking "Take yer hands out of yer pockets boy !", school
dinners, figs and lumpy custard, the smell of over-cooked
cabbage....spuds.

Spud Taylor !

I screw the paper into a tiny ball.

SLEEPING ROUGH SLEEPIN PARK

The 21st century
and here I am living
like a fucking
cave-man.

Just recently I've started seriously
thinking of topping myself...
Like a silly cunt, I thought
of hiring a car.

I needed ninety quid to hire one
for the weekend so I could do
a proper job, but how could I,
I haven't got a pot to piss in.

So I said "Fuck it."
I've just had a half-cup
of coffee today -
I tried a Hostel once.

Well, that really did mi head in
I remember that first night.
There was this head-banging
bastard banging on mi bedroom

door, shouting;
*"Nan Noo Nan Noo
  Nan Noo Nan Noo."*
He'd been sniffing glue.

Who wants to stay in some
Poxy little room anyway ?
Some of the people in 'em are more
Mental than me.......

Just recently, I went to see
Mi mam - she looked at me
As if to say
Who the fuck are you ?

THE TENANCIES

My good neighbour
uses illnesses like
a weapon, ringing
the nurse, involving
her husband. Too
much noise; singing,
washing, blocking
her view, doors
slamming, someone
talking back.
It makes her ILL, ILL.
Incest and drink
are a big problem
at number two.
(Mother and Son ;
innocent, inoffensive.)
At number three
two young journalists
left overnight:
"Prostitutes !" she said.
So now I fear
the watcher;
the flick of curtains,
being on the list -
my beard, my guitar,
all that Jazz FM.
I smile too much.
Classification :
Squinty-eyed
Smack Head.

The sweet smell
of honeysuckle
draws my grandchild
to your garden.
You, banging
on my door,
disturbs my Sunday
siesta, my good neighbour.
Your cheesegrater face
fucking hates kids.
Try to calm you down,
offer you sweet tea.
You slam the door,
my two-year-old cries.
You bake cakes
for the landlord -
he thinks you are nice,
typical landlord -
a bit of a cunt.
Wasps fly
around your
sugary apple pies.

NEARLY SIXTY, PLAYING SQUASH

A young girlfriend made him feel good.
Ten months later, a one-month-old kid.
She'd got two already, four - five years old.

He wished he'd had his balls chopped off.
His wife kicked him out; he'd done it before.
That was the last straw.

He's locked in his room one flight up.
Surrounded. His classical records, his books.
He reads one on poisons to music by Strauss.

His newly-acquired children are screaming outside.
Strauss suddenly turned up.

SHOTS ON TARGET

He knew there was something wrong
when she started putting seasonal
decorations up during Euro '96.

Things came to a head
when she was making some royal icing
for the Christmas cake.

He was shouting and clapping as
Shearer had just scored a goal.
Bing Crosby was singing his famous festive song

over and over on the CD in the kitchen.
He turned the TV up and you could hear
the whole stadium.

"You're a bastard!" she said
to the top of his head
and let him have both barrels.

DIS MORNING DIS VOICE SEZ

Forget der training, go and make yerself
a bacon sarni, dip up der fat,
slop on der brown sauce, fuck der training.

I've gotta build up dis body eat der right foods
train der mind, like when I see a cracking
burd walking down der street, dis voice
always sez yer gotta shag the arse off dat burd.
I gotta fink dat cud be someone else's burd.

How wud I feel someone shagging der arse off my burd ?

LOVE AND MARRIAGE

First day of the January Sales
and here we are bumper to bumper town centre,
missed the turn off for the car park three times
causing a blazing row.
I tell her I've lost my bottle when it comes to heavy traffic
secretly wishing I'd never come in the first place.
Then I'll leave her to carry on with the shopping
and I'll spend the first half of the day
browsing in Waterstones,
second half at the Harris Museum
and that I'll meet her at 5 o'clock outside Pizza Hut.
"Stop the bloody car, NOW !" she says.
"Listen," I say, "I've taken this shit for thirty years !"
She tries to get out, but we go round endlessly
in the swirl of a roundabout.

MOTH

Moth moves into the cup's shadow
where the light won't hurt him;
we find him a darker place.

Everything seems okay
our vegetarian dishes,
the ersatz chicken and bacon.

The Barolo and Chablis go down well.
We are with a charming couple
'til they talk about films

the original uncut version
of *The Texas Chain Saw Massacre*.
About the boiled-up pet rabbit

in the movie *Fatal Attraction*.
About a black and white video
they watch over and over

small monkeys having the tops of their skulls
pushed through holes in special tables
where they are sliced off, their brains eaten.

Afterwards, when they have gone
we release the oak-coloured moth
into a night bathing with moonlight.

Talk about butterflies in warm meadows
about the red air balloon we saw
gently rising above dark woods.

NIGHT COACH

My feet are swollen
and I cannot sleep.
My eyes are awash with blue
neon and night lights.
Outside these moving windows
people are sleeping peacefully.
Some are in the Chapel of Rest.
Babies are being born.
Someone's crying over a death.
Girls with long black hair
and olive skin are dreaming,
hiding eyes that can stun
at twenty paces.

I wake from day dreams
though it's dusky dark
as we rise above lake Garda
the shore lights glittering.
From a distance
an electric golden cross
seems to hover in thin air.
It leaves a meaningful
and desired effect upon me
as if the Lord had washed my feet.

Suddenly, and without warning
we race through a long tunnel;
an Italian Samba playing.
Our coach driver seems to dance
as the tunnel lights
create a strobe effect :
Maybe it's their trick
but he seems to be moving
into the rhythm
like a raving demon
like a jockey whipping
a wild-eyed horse
as we thunder on.

TOO MANY WINTERS

You want a young man
who can smother you
in milk and honey;
can take you to the moon
buck like a rodeo bronc;
wrap you in his mane
cover you in stardust.

You don't want me;
a man who's seen
too many blizzards.
Fingers burnt to the bone,
tears freezing as they fall -
my sun as weak as moonlight
my bed a slab of marble.

MAYBE

Maybe someone didn't like the song
reminded them of a love affair
gone sour or the shape of the guitar.

Maybe someone had been singing
about the forgotten and the lonely
triggered a moment of madness;

hands coming from nowhere,
splintering to pieces in five seconds.
Broken frets, broken lives ?

Anyhow, there'll be no more moonlight
serenades with A majors or E minors
fingers working a blues riff.

THE TOILET SEAT

The toilet seat, she says,
I know who's leaving it up !

Does it matter about the seat,
I say, whether it's up or down ?

When the front door's open, she says,
that's the first thing people see.

The toilet seat, it looks
much better when it's down.

Does it really matter, I say.
Of course it matters, she says,

nothing looks worse.
So, you mean, I say, that everyone

walking down the street,
just happens to be hoping

that the front door's open,
so that they can see

the toilet seat's up ?
It's not just that, she says,

it's if anyone calls to see us too;
it looks unsightly.

Why don't we close
the toilet door then ?

I was coming to that,
she replies.

TITCH

Here we are in a charity shop.
We spend a lot of our days
in them, me poking
around for poetry books.

It's quite amazing really
what you can find for 29 pence
a couple of big press names;
soon out of fashion
but that's okay by me.
58 pence for the two
is just within my price range.

Titch, my wife, buy's another Pot-Cat,
Christ, we've a full house already !

Anyway, I'm happy with what
I've bought, in fact,
it's made my day.

She roots through some Catherine Cookson. I'm sure
she's read all her books by now
I sit in the one solitary
chair provided, start to read.

"Come on. Are you going
to stay there all day ?" she asks.

Are you for sale ?

TOM

It's my turn to look after Tom.
Bleary-eyed I come downstairs.
Already, he is trying to shove
Tom and Jerry into the video
but in the end we have
two minutes of "don't like",
Jungle Book, The Lion King,
Peter Pan, finally settling on
Bob the Builder; in between
we've had cheese smeared
on the settee, coffee knocked
down the back of the telly,
a stubbed toe, the cat
running up the curtain.

BEFORE TEA

Life's real all right.
Titch relaxes on our couch.
I give her the Daily Paper.
Within a couple of minutes
she starts to cry.

There's a nice piece
of haddock on a plate
in our fridge.
Freshly cut chips
submerged in water.

He was only three
and they shot him
in the head at point blank
range, because he said
his nose was itchy, she says.

Peas have soaked
overnight in a bowl.
And the bread is still
warm from Safeway.

YOU WORK ON THE NIGHTSHIFT

The weekend. I've just got to say one word
out of line and it's argument time.
I don't blame you, it's just the way things are.
"Where's your brains ?" you say.
Trying to align ourselves, come to grips
with the situation; a continual battle
of trying to get some equilibrium,
your big problem not knowing
whether you're on your head or arse,
like not being able to tell the moon from the sun.
Let's face it, we're completely two different species
trying to be compatible, sympathetic.
Sometimes by a miracle we get it right,
and smile at each other from across the table.

W A R

Three guys wearing baseball caps,
wielding baseball bats, jumped out
of this MR2 late last night,
music on full blast.

Boom ! Boom ! Boom !

Smashing the car across the street -
windscreen-windows-lights.

Boom ! Boom ! Boom !

All done and dusted in a few seconds,
then off into the night like a fucking war-canoe.
It's getting like the streets of San Francisco.

Who are those people over the road ?

LAUGHING POLICEMAN

Have you ever been beaten up ?
Only once, I say, in a back-alley,
a dustbin fell on top of me
during the fight,
then the assailant really stuck
the boot in, knocked seven-bells
out of me. How terrible,
they say. I am beginning
to feel uncomfortable
because I am no longer policing
the cinema - I'm sat talking,
one ear cocked for the sergeant,
helmet pushed back.

In a row of seats to the left
five or six policemen
start to barrack me -
one's telling the whole cinema
it's my first day on duty,
I'm feeling quite smug because
I know I'm a pseudo-policeman.

I start walking down the aisle,
my uniform's becoming too large,
drops off like a second skin;
it's like nightfall.

THE CHIPPY

So. Ordering haddock, chips, and peas twice
I stand and wait and a young girl
in the queue tells me she's been up
since six a.m. nursing two kittens who have no mother.

She yawns; waits for her chicken nuggets.
I look at her tiny frame, her sloping shoulders;
think of the old black and white postcards -
Victorian children of Heptonstall playing
leap-frog outside the sweet shop

'til the scent of palm oil, fish and chips
pulls me back, seeing one of the men in the shop
evenly basting the strips of cod and haddock
with a cream of batter, gliding it
with a fish fryer's ease into hot, sizzling oil.

Not far away two kittens paw a ball of wool
stabbed with needles. In the churchyard
she lies resting; above her a circle
of small stones. Night draws in.

GLASS

Frank was once a dapper man on the fast track
had the ears of the board, the keys to a Porsche,
the hand of an Angel wearing his wedding ring.
A detached five-bedroom out in the suburbs -
I give him loose change, wish him well -
"And to you, good sir," he says.
I'd seen him before meandering between traffic lights.
This time I called his name, there's no weight to him,
no backside, if I hadn't smelt alcohol, I'd have thought
he had cancer, the full face gone, the light of life
no longer in the eyes. I leave him sharing a bottle
with friends; sitting on broken glass, on the Town Hall
    steps.
Pigeons are being fed by an old lady wearing a woolly hat,
an over-sized coat in the full heat of this summer day.

THE SWEATER

Here I am getting petrol,
when this blonde about thirty
draws up in a white limousine.
She's got that smudged lipstick look.
She gets out, leans over to undo
the petrol cap, pushes the nozzle
to the hilt, pumps it.

My eyes lock on her huge breasts
hanging inside her red sweater,
her small waist accentuating
them even more. Her legs are long
and sensual, shiny high heels
and a little black dress, suits me well.

She stuns me with a crooked smile;
sees the dog in my eyes.

The first reading
I ever did was at Fleetwood library.
Three old ladies turned up....
(not that I've got anything against old ladies)
One fell asleep, one gazed out of the window.
At the end I decided to put some zing into it,
sing, play my guitar; *Proud Mary,*
Johnny Be Good, Blowing in the Wind.
The last old lady gave me a clap;
CLAP ! CLAP !

Said, *"Do you do Danny Boy ?"*

HEY MAN!

Went along to this poetry appreciation group
that a friend told me about. Evidently everyone
takes a couple of poems which they read out in turn;
open discussion follows. Anyway, when it comes
to my poems Kenneth Koch, Ashbury, silence follows.

"Clap yer feet and stamp yer hands !" I shout,
before I do a Blues Brothers cartwheel right outta the place.

THE LECTURER

Thought he was an undiscovered Ezra Pound.
Loved himself when he read Antony and Cleopatra

to a captive audience of twelve;
when it came to Caesar we need an umbrella.

I tried to show him a new anthology, today's poetry.
Crap, he said, *it says nothin', it's going nowhere.*

Now, let me tell you about some real poets,
he said, putting his arm around my shoulder.

LIAM

Thought he was Bukowski
Lenny Bruce and Jerry Lewis
all rolled into one;
in fact a real cool dude.
A pony-tailed Poet in Residence
Shagging all the little girls
(who knew no fucking better
but soon would) reading them
his poems in bed, saying
they were really deep.
There's too many dickheads
writing these days he sez.

THE PARTY

I know you're getting somewhere
with your poetry
but please don't become one
of those boring bastards

and don't start thinking
you're Philip Larkin
or even Shelley or Keats
you may laugh

but I saw you
wrapping yourself round a tree
at the barbie
at the poetry party

like you were a vine
like you were a tortured soul
like you were fucking Dylan Thomas
or something

during that rainfall
that thunderstorm last July.
If you're not careful
you'll be doing a Ph.D.
in English Literature

and bragging about it.

HE DOESN'T SEE ME
ON THE CAMPUS CAR PARK

He hums constantly he's of slight build
a little hunchbacked wears tortoise shell glasses
hair plastered down neat parting
he repeatedly looks at this brown envelope
keeps putting it back in his pocket
patting the pocket it's in still humming
He bounces as he walks he gets to the car
parked next to mine he doesn't see me
pulls out the envelope takes a key out of it
He hums smiles and holds it up to the sun
then puts it back into the envelope
takes it out and puts it back
does this at least six times
Repeats the procedure of putting it in his pocket
patting it and taking it out and putting it back
Then he takes off his jacket and puts it in the boot
of his car locks it opens it and puts the jacket
back on hums takes out the envelope and

KNIGHTWOOD (1)

When they go through the handing out sweets ritual
it's as if they walk through her
it's as if she doesn't exist no-one talks to her.
She wants to die, in fact, most times she wants to
at 4 a.m. it's icy cold nothing keeps her warm.
Every minute's an hour no-one talks to her.
One smile could save her no-one talks to her.
The line pounds in her ears no-one talks to her.

KNIGHTWOOD (2)

I hate this fucking job.
So do I, I'm just hoping I'll win the lottery.
You'll never fucking win it, it's those cunts
who love the fucking job who'll win it,
not the fucking likes of you and me
who fucking hate the bastard job,
both together now we love the job, we love the job
we love the job we love the job....

THUNDER

He walks with a real strut
nearly straight as a die -
but with a slight lean
as if any minute he'll topple over.
He wears boots with silver-tips,
has a small gleaming diamond
set amongst perfect teeth.

Most of the time he's working
on machines that break down.
Loud music from Rock FM
thumps out over the lines,
when *Prince* comes on, there's
a real rhythm in his step,
twirling massive spanners
up in the air like a juggler.

I overheard him say, "Prince
is the only guy I'd ever sleep with
I'd do anything he wanted."
Anyway here I am trying
to put pink plastic caps
on fast moving lines of hairspray cans.

He's right behind me like Satan
himself, sat on top of a stacked palette
cross-legged; giving me the Evils.
Now, for someone like me
who's new to the job
it's very unsettling.

"It took me 18 months to get used
to capping," says Billy who's working
on the line with me,
"So, don't take fuck-all notice of Psycho Joe
there; he'd be doing time, if it wasn't
for his Uncle being the Boss !"

DAYLIGHT ROBBERY

10 years on the night-shift hasn't been easy for Titch.
She doesn't foul mouth like the rest, in fact she has
nothing in common with her workmates.
Except from the first few years of falling prey
to being the butt of their continual jokes and jibes.

Titch's seen those with lesser strengths soon part company.
Over a period of time, she's been accepted
as part of the scenery; the hum-drum lines,
the boredom, the clocking in and out.

This year they gave her a birthday card.

GIVE A DOG A NAME

He started asking her questions, personal questions, hadn't
    she had enough,
it had been five years since she had lost her business, her
    home.
She was stuck in this job, she'd no choice there wasn't much
    else left.
She'd picked herself up and now this dickhead of a kid was
    shouting at her,
"What's it like to be bankrupt ?" telling the whole bastard
    world; the factory.
Like a dog with a bone, didn't people ever let things drop ?

She felt like moving to a new town, even changing her
    name,
but why should she; she's worked hard, all her life,
lost everything through no fault of her own, for trying to
    do her best.
And here was this gangly twenty-two year old half-mad,
    half-stupid,
like most of the world. She wanted to stick him with a knife

but she just asked to be moved to another line.
She knew life would fuck this toe-rag one way or another.

SLOGGING HER GUTS OUT

Keeping her head down, being a good girl.
"Work hard," she could hear her mother saying

"and you'll always come good."
She could do with the extra money,

what with her husband's breakdown.
She knew he'd never work again

just like a child now
one who'd never ever leave her.

A small step up the ladder would help
but always came the bimbos

putting on their little girl acts
covered in make-up, all tits and arse

sharing the line leader's soup
pinching the boys' bums

building up their fragile egos
giving out hand-jobs like humbugs.

They infiltrate the whole system
in Administration, Quality Control,

on the line, all helping to fuck up
any kind of promotion

for years and years to come.

SPIELER

There have been hard working conscientious people
in this place for years who will never see promotion.
But the management of Knightwood Factory never cease
to entertain us with their gullibility, because this week
we've got Freda with the figure who's been here twelve
  months.

"I'm your new supervisor," she tells everyone at the
  meeting.
"I expect full co-operation off everybody, I've been
part of top-flight management. I've run various companies."

She times everyone going to the toilet.

STRAWBERRIES

She remembers the first time
her husband said, "Will you marry me ?"
She told her friends at work *that's it.*
Summers of champagne and strawberries
followed, croquet and boule on the lawn.
Four or five holidays a year.
But then things changed; like they often do.
Her husband's inability to hold on
to the family business.

Afterwards moving in with an eighteen stone
school mistress, who he met at assertion classes
run by the W.E.A. :
She remembers a friend telling her she once
knew her and bragged openly
about knowing every position
in the Kama Sutra.

Now here she was at Knightwood Factory.
Divorced.
Working on the lines.
"I'm only doing this job
because it's part of my research
for the book I'm writing,"
she says to someone on the line
who doesn't give a fuck anyway.

JOE

Joe is used to being spat on.
Being called all the names under the sun.
He sweeps up metal shavings all day long.
Workers piss in his orange in the fridge.
Steal the Westerns that he loves to read.
Hide his bicycle the next twenty years.
He will walk home in the slanting rain
taking it all in his stride.
It makes them feel better
as if they are torturing themselves.
He will return to his flat night after night
be tormented as much in dreams
as he is in his working hours.
Joe will die of a heart attack six weeks
after retiring, there will be no bouquets,
the earth will not move.
The dog he wanted will not keep vigil.

THE CAGE

He's coming towards the end of another 12 hours
with a sore throat, headache from the noise
of the machines, tiredness through every bone,
as he buttons hair-spray cans that arrive at speed
some sadist bastard has set to meet demands.

Six hard buttons held in each hand simultaneously
scooped from a tray fed by hoppers through the ceiling -
seeds to a bird, thumbs and forefingers working away,
connecting buttons to cans that hiss spray
as if cooling burns.

Printed & bound by
BEACON DM
Unit 2, Valley Road Business Park
Gas Works Road
Keighley
BD21 4LY

Tel. 0 1 5 3 5 6 8 0 3 8 1
Fax. 0 1 5 3 5 6 6 4 6 6 1